SEARCHING
AMERICAN MILITARY
RECORDS

SEARCHING AMERICAN MILITARY RECORDS

By
FRAN CARTER

AGLL
Bountiful, Utah
1996

American Genealogical Lending Library
P.O. Box 329, Bountiful, UT 84010-329

Printed in the United States of America
99 98 97 96   8 7 6 5 4 3

ISBN 0-945433-28-X

CONTENTS

CONTENTS

INTRODUCTION

Many of our ancestors have been involved in some sort of military action in the service of our country. Often we need to make some educated guesses and analyze dates and places where our ancestors lived in order to isolate the probability of this service. We may need to remind ourselves of the dates military conflicts occurred. The question most important to be asked about our ancestors (especially males) is, "Would they have been of an age to serve in the military at the time a particular conflict occurred?" When the answer is yes — and many times it will be — we can ask ourselves: What records were created *then?* Where can I locate those records *now?* And what information would those records contain that might answer my particular genealogical questions?

There are many types of military records which might contain genealogical information important to your research. These records were created from the earliest times in the history of our country and are still being created. Most information from pre-Revolutionary War military records can be found in books found in genealogical collections throughout the country. These will be discussed later in this work. The intent of this book is to get you thinking about what happened, when, what caused military records to be created, and where you can find those records today.

The inalienable rights of *"life, liberty and the pursuit of happiness"* were more stirring words when first heard by young men in the Revolutionary War period of our history of our country than perhaps they are today. Many of these young men volunteered for military service in what was an untested and loosely organized group of military personnel in the fight for independence against a mighty and majestic army of Great Britain. We should not lose sight of this fact when thinking of military service for our ancestors. It has great bearing on the life and acts of these brave young men.

From pre-Revolutionary War times military records have been kept. They contain facts relating to births, deaths, marriages, and other family relationships. The records become very valuable to us as we pursue our genealogy research.

WHERE TO LOCATE MILITARY RECORDS

Records pertaining to the federal government are in the custody of the National Archives. Since 1941 the National Archives has microfilmed federal records of high research interest to make the records available for researchers while preserving the originals from deterioration and damage from handling. Copies of these microfilmed records are sold to the public, making these federal records accessible to libraries, research centers, and individuals.

Major sources for copies of the microfilmed military records are the American Genealogical Lending Library (AGLL) and the LDS Family History Centers (FHL).

NATIONAL ARCHIVES

One can visit the National Archives in Washington D.C. or any of its branches throughout the country. Once an ancestor has been identified and you know which war in which he served, you can send to the archives for a copy of the information. The current price is $10.00 per file. One should specify the war and the name of the person who served. You will need a proper form obtained from the Archives before this mail search is begun.

AGLL

Military records can be rented or purchased from the American Genealogical Lending Library, P.O. Box 244, Bountiful, UT 84011. The telephone number is (801) 298-5358. AGLL is a privately owned company which offers membership to individuals for a small fee and supplies microfilm to public libraries on interlibary loan. Your local library may already use their services. AGLL owns many of the military records on microfilm. These can be requested for use in your home or library and read at your leisure. The cost is minimal. AGLL also rents or sells microfilm and microfiche of more than 100,000 titles including ship passenger lists, censuses, state and county records, and printed genealogies.

The current catalog is quite extensive on military records. For the Revolutionary War they have the Pension and Bounty Land Warrant Application files, the Compiled Service Records, and Compiled Service Record Index. The Compiled Service Records and/or Indexes are also available for soldiers who served from 1784-188, War of 1812, various Indian Wars, Civil War, and other wars from 1866 to the end of the nineteenth century.

FAMILY HISTORY LIBRARY

The Family History Library (Salt Lake City, Utah) and over 2,000 of its Family History Centers throughout the world also have copies of the National Archives military records. These can be viewed at the main library in Salt Lake. They may also be ordered from the Family History Center in your home town and viewed at their facilities for a nominal cost. Indexes are available for many of the military records mentioned in this book and may be obtained in the same manner.

COUNTY RECORDS

Applications for pensions and bounty land warrants are often initiated at the local level of jurisdiction — the County Court. One might find a local court minute book filled with applications made at this level before being sent to Washington and eventually filed with the National Archives.

My great grandmother made her first application for a widow's and dependent's pension (Civil War) at the courthouse in Johnson County, Missouri, where she lived at the time. She presented all documentation and signed a power of attorney for a representative to present her case in Washington, D.C. When this application was denied, she went to the adjoining county of Pettis and filed another application, following the same procedures, presenting the same documents, and again was denied. "Never give up" may have started as the family motto at this time. She tried again in Saline County (another adjoining county). This time it was approved. She was granted a widow's pension and two children's pensions for her two youngest children until they reached 18 years of age. Each county had copies of birth, marriage, death, and relationships in their records. The same records were only alluded to at the National Archives in their records.

All three counties have copies of the same documents. Johnson County, where she lived, also recorded an annual report to the pension bureau as long as the children remained under the age of 18. Then she filed a final report for them and continued to receive her monthly pension ($8.00) until her death in 1922.

STATE RECORDS

No set pattern seems to exist for what STATE records were kept. When they do exist, they seem to follow the same pattern of the National Archives collection — except the men registered are from one particular state. These might be found in the state archives, historical societies, museums, and created/donated collections within a specific state.

LOCAL MILITIA RECORDS

On 8 May 1792, Congress authorized a state enrollment of all able-bodied free white males, aged 18 to 45, to combat Indian uprisings in the Northwest Territory. Local militia had existed before this time to defend the local area where the enrolled men resided. These militia men were called out periodically for drills and exercises but served only in times of emergency. These were not necessarily professional soldiers but local farmers and businessmen organized to protect their local territories. Militia records might be found in local county court records, private records, historical collections, museums, etc.

4

OUR COUNTRY'S WARS

For genealogical study, let's divide the various wars and conflicts into categories and time periods. This may help us with our chronological study and help us place our ancestor in an age group which could have served.

COLONIAL WARS

The American Colonial Period produced at least *some* records of military engagements. Many of these early colonial war records might be found in privately published sources, in book form, periodicals, pamphlets, etc.

PEQUOT WAR (1636-1637)

Admittedly this was an unofficial war, but apparently well researched and documented in *A Scattered People* by Gerald McFarland. The book describes a tragic series of communication breakdowns which were blown out of proportion and which started the war. Land was plentiful in Connecticut. A Pequot Indian had cleared a plot of ground for his livestock, but left it temporarily because of an outbreak of smallpox. He drove his cattle off and took his family away to avoid the plague.

While the Pequot and his cattle were gone, John Endicott filed claim to the land that had been "abandoned." Violence erupted. The settlers set fire to a large Indian stronghold in the middle of the night. All the Pequot Indians who attempted to flee from the burning structures were murdered. Those who remained were cremated alive. Four to six hundred Indian men, women and children were killed. Two white settlers lost their lives. Thus started and ended a two year skirmish with the Pequot Indians. Many settlers of the area fought in this war.

KING WILLIAM'S WAR (1689-1697)

Many of the men who were involved in this conflict of land and naval forces came from the New England States. The war was a battle between English and French forces and was fought from the Mohawk River to the St. Lawrence River.

The treaty of Ryswick, 30 Sept 1697, restored some order to the colonies and turned this Hudson Bay dispute over to the commissioners who reached no agreement. In England this war is also known as the "War of the League of Augsburg" and records are filed under that name. Mostly New England residents fought in this early war.

QUEEN ANNE'S WAR (1744-1748)

Sometimes this was is called the "War of Spanish Succession." This was a European war with only a few colonists participating. Most of these people were from the New England States and enrolled in sea oriented services. There were some battles in Maine, and in Deerfield, Massachusetts. Under the Treaty of Utrecht in 1713, Britain secured Nova Scotia, Newfoundland, and the Hudson Bay regions. One might search records of these localities for participants in militia as well as naval activities.

WAR OF JENKIN'S EAR (1739-1742)

The name is not misleading. Over alleged mistreatment of a merchant seaman (notably Robert Jenkins) and other hostile acts, England declared war on Spain. Some seamen from the Colonies were involved inn battles near St. Simon's Island and St. Augustine. To find information, try printed records first, then seamen records.

KING GEORGE'S WAR (1744-1748)

This war of Austrian succession included early colonists who answered the call for soldiers. Fought almost entirely in Europe, but some colonists did serve.

FRENCH AND INDIAN WARS (1754-1763)

Sometimes this war is called the "Seven Years War." The primary cause was conflict between Virginia and France for command of the upper Ohio River, especially the forks of the Ohio where the French had built Fort Duquesne (present day

Pittsburgh). During this war the colonists served in British Service. Whole units served, but most soldiers never received compensation from the English. For records of troops be sure to search histories of the areas where the fighting took place instead of histories of the persons' home towns. Histories of battle areas often contain names of persons who fought there.

PONTIAC'S REBELLION (1763-1764)

A colonial war — short, yet vicious — which involved colonists from the border areas of Pennsylvania, Maryland, Virginia, and adjoining colonies. This war opened the way for settlement of the west.

REVOLUTIONARY WAR (1764-1775)

The American Revolution — the birth of a new nation — resulted in awards to any person who served in this conflict. Bounty lands were rewarded to many surviving veterans which led to the movement of many of our ancestors to the frontier areas. The long period of war for independence involved most of the men of military age and created the *first* records for a new nation. These will be discussed later in detail.

POST-REVOLUTIONARY WARS

NAVAL WAR WITH FRANCE (1798-1800)

Sometimes called the "Tripolitian War," this war was an undeclared navel conflict over the shipping trade. Many of our seamen served in this naval conflict.

BARBARY WAR (1801-1804)

This war involved mostly Naval units and pirates of the Barbary States of North Africa. Try seamen records.

WAR OF 1812 (1812-1815)

Sometimes this war is referred to as the "Second War of Independence from England." Many of our ancestors performed military service during this war and received compensation.

INDIAN WARS (18TH AND 19TH CENTURIES)

During early colonial times, Indian wars were called skirmishes and fought by local militia men and women within the villages involved. Records were probably never made. During the 19th century, skirmishes and full-scale wars between whites and Indians occurred. Records may be found in:

* State Archives where soldier, or civilian fought.
* National Archives for soldiers who fought in federal service.
* County Records for local skirmishes.
* Printed histories of battles.
* Museums, historical collections, private collections, military histories, etc.

SEMINOLE WAR (FIRST 1817-1818; SECOND 1835-1842; THIRD 1856-1858)

Troops for this war with the Seminole Indians of Florida came from many states in the union. Data and records might be obtained from the National Archives for soldiers fighting in federal service. For county service, check the local county records.

MEXICAN WAR (1846-1848)

The war with Mexico involved troops from nearly every state in the Union. Many men received military bounty lands in partial payment for these services. Again, records at the *federal* level would be found with the National Archives.

THE CIVIL WAR *OR* THE WAR OF THE REBELLION*OR*

THE WAR BETWEEN THE STATES (1861-1865)

Volumes of information can be found on the Civil War and the soldiers who fought both for the North and the South. The records of this conflict will be discussed in more detail in a separate section.

HAWAII WAR (1893)

United States marines aided the Revolutionary Committee of Safety to overthrow the native government of Hawaii. Annexation was accomplished in 1898. Military records for this war are found in the National Archives. Soldiers from most states were involved.

SPANISH AMERICAN WAR (1898-1901)

This war between the United States and Spain found both volunteer and regular troops serving from nearly every state in the union. Amazingly enough, though many men served, few genealogists check these records. Records are found at the National Archives.

PHILIPPINE INSURRECTION (1899-1902)

Sometimes this war is considered a continuation of the Spanish American War. This is a misconception as Spain was not involved. Records of men who served may be found in both the National Archives and various state archives, since state military units were used as well as federal troops.

BOXER REBELLION (1899-1902)

This was a Chinese revolt put down by international forces including the United States' regular troops [mostly enlisted men]. Consult the National Archives for these records.

WAR WITH PANAMA (1903)

Columbia rejected a proposal to relinquish control over the Panama Canal Zone. When war broke out, the United States government recognized the Republic of Panama as a country. Records were created for regular troops. Records are at both the National Archives and state archives for these troops.

DOMINICAN REPUBLIC WAR (1904)

When this Caribbean country failed to meet debts owed to the United States and foreign creditors, the United States government exercised "police" powers in this action. Check the National Archives for records.

NICARAGUA (1911)

United States Marines landed in Nicaragua to protect American interests in 1911. A small group remained until 1933. Records are at the National Archives.

WAR WITH MEXICO (1914)

United States forces arrived on Mexican soil in 1914 and caused the Mexican dictator to abdicate. The United States Army and Navy were involved. Check the National Archives for records of this conflict.

HAITI (1915)

Military troops occupied Haiti and were not totally withdrawn until 1934. Records for federal troops are at the National Archives.

MEXICO (1916)

In 1916 United States troops were once again involved in Mexico. Troops were withdrawn when war with Germany seemed imminent. Check the National Archives for records.

WORLD WAR I (1914-1918)

This was "the war to end all wars." United States involvement in this European war was extensive. Many records exist. Records of volunteers and drafted men and women are at the National Archives, state archives, local museums, historical libraries, and in numerous printed histories and lists.

WORLD WAR II (1939-1945)

Volunteers and drafted men and women served in this war. Records exist at the National Archives, regional archives, state archives, state court systems, in printed lists, memorials, museums and historical libraries, etc. All sorts of materials exist on people who served in this war.

KOREAN WAR (1950-1953)

This is the first war sanctioned by the United Nations. The United States furnished most of the allied forces in this war. The

10

National Archives has records. Direct descendancy needs to be proven to obtain these records.

LEBANON (1958-1983)

The United States was involved with international police force action. Terrorist bombing started the melée. Records are at the National Archives.

DOMINICAN REPUBLIC (1965)

United States Troops remained here over one year creating the Inter-American Peace Force.

VIETNAM (1954-1973)

The longest war in United States history started with economic and technical assistance and intensified into a major conflict. It spanned the administration of five presidents. Records are at the National Archives, at war memorials, etc.

GRENADA (1983)

A military coup in Grenada brought the intervention of United States troops [two months involvement]. Records are kept in the National Archives.

DESERT STORM (1990-1991)

Iraq's invasion of Kuwait brought allied coalition troops to repel Iraq's forces and back them into their own territory. Many military personnel were involved. Records are found in the National Archives.

NATIONAL ARCHIVES

The National Archives and Records Administration, the official title used and abbreviated as N.A.R.A., was established in 1934. It was first administered under the General Services Administration until about 1985. Currently it is being directed under one National Archivist who reports directly to the President of the United States.

The Archives buildings include a large building in Washington and an annex in Alexandria, Virginia, nine Presidential Libraries, eleven regional libraries established in 1969, and thirteen record centers. They house the following materials:

* Original Documents (called textual records)
* Photographs
* Maps
* Drawings
* Magnetic Tapes
* Motion Pictures
* Census Returns
* Military Service, Pension Files, Bounty Land Warrants
* Immigration Records
* Ships Passenger Lists
* Other records

The National Archives and Records Administration was created to manage *noncurrent* records created by *federal agencies,* as well as the Legislative, Judicial, and Executive branches of the United States government. The National Archives staff and the National Archivist make decisions on what to keep and inventory, and develop descriptive finding aids for this massive collection. This staff also categorizes the records, preserves them, and makes them available for public use.

An attempt is made to keep the records in the form in which they were created and not rearrange them. Thus they are arranged by Record Group. This groups them together according to the agency which created them.

Filming of these records makes the searching much easier. This filming began in 1941 and continues today. The most sought after records were filmed first. Remember they were filmed in Record Groups. This may be important to you later.

Microfilm publication numbers are assigned to each microfilm publication. These are preceded by M, T, or A. M is for an entire series of records. At the beginning of the first roll, an introduction is reproduced that contains explanatory material. Many M series publications have printed descriptive pamphlets available from the National Archives. These are free for the asking.

T and A series publications do not always contain a complete set of records. These T and A series may have been filmed in segments, by date or subject, or even acquired in film format from other agencies. They are reproduced and/or sold exactly as filmed. Also, T and A series do not have introductions or descriptive pamphlets printed about them.

The National Archives and Records Administration in Washington, D.C. publishes *Microfilm Resources for Research: A Comprehensive Catalog*. The microfilm publication information is arranged by numbered record group according to the agency that created them. This is generally at the bureau level. Within each group, the microfilm publications are arranged to make them easy to use.

The National Archives is the official repository for records of military *personnel* who have been discharged from the United States Army, Air Force, Marines, and Navy. The main repository is in Washington, D.C. The optimum search method is to go there in person and see the actual papers. These records have been filmed They are available to us in many locations. Check the major library collections.

REGIONAL BRANCHES OF THE NATIONAL ARCHIVES

Regional branches of the National Archives were established in 1969. They were created to help alleviate the burden of the National Archives staff in Washington, D. C. and to expand the space for storage of materials particular to each region. Copies were made of selected film titles held at the National Archives and placed in these regional branches. Thus we have materials available to us in our regions. The regional branches house the following materials:

* All available federal censuses, 1790 - 1920
* All available census soundex film, 1880-1920 (soundex or miracode for 21 states in 1910)
* Military records for most wars
* Union veterans, and widows of veterans enumerated in the 1890 census (118 rolls of film)
* Published census indexes (in most branches)

NATIONAL ARCHIVES FIELD BRANCHES AND THE AREAS SERVED

Atlanta Field Branch
1557 St. Joseph Avenue
East Point, GA 30340
(Alabama, Georgia, Florida, Kentucky, Mississippi, North Carolina, Tennessee)

Boston Field Branch
380 Trapelo Road
Waltham, MA 02154
(Connecticut, Maine, Massachusetts, New Hampshire, Rhode Island, Vermont)

Chicago Field Branch
7358 South Pulaski Road
Chicago, IL 60629
(Illinois, Indiana, Michigan, Minnesota, Ohio, Wisconsin)

14

Denver Field Branch
Building 48, Denver Federal Center
Denver, CO 80225
(Colorado, Montana, North Dakota, South Dakota, Utah,
Wyoming)

Fort Worth Field Branch
501 West Felix Street
Fort Worth, TX 76115
(Arkansas, Louisiana, New Mexico, Oklahoma, Texas)

Kansas City Field Branch
2312 East Bannister Road
Kansas City, MO 64131
(Iowa, Kansas, Missouri, Nebraska)

Los Angeles Field Branch
24000 Avila Road
P. O. Box 6719
Los Angeles, CA 90086
(Arizona, plus Southern California counties of Imperial, Inyo,
Kern, Los Angeles, Orange, Riverside, San Bernadino, San
Louis Obispo, Santa Barbara, and Ventura. Also Clark
County, Nevada)

New York Field Branch
Building 22, Mot Bayonne
Bayonne, NJ 07002
(New Jersey, New York, Puerto Rico, and Virgin Islands)

Philadelphia Field Branch
9th and Market Street, Room 1350
Philadelphia, PA 19107
(Pennsylvania, Maryland, Virginia, West Virginia)

San Francisco Field Branch
1000 Commodore Drive
San Bruno, CA 94066
(Hawaii, Northern California, the Pacific Ocean area, and
Nevada except Clark County)

Seattle Field Branch
6125 Sand Point Way, North East
Seattle, WA 98115
(Alaska, Idaho, Oregon, Washington)

MILITARY RECORDS CATEGORIES IN THE NATIONAL ARCHIVES

Military records are divided into separate categories in the National Archives system of recording.

<u>Service Records</u> may contain records of where the person served, when and where he or she was inducted and discharged, affidavits fellow soldiers, names of people served under, units served in, battles participated in, rank, possible aliases, promotions or demotions, pay, personal description, language(s) spoken, etc. In other words, the records contain all information concerning the service for a particular person at a particular time.

<u>Pension Records</u> may contain any application for pension by the service person or his spouse whether granted or denied. Records may contain names (often maiden name of wife), date married, complete description of soldier, dates and place of service, persons served with and under, children or dependents, places of residence, injuries suffered in service, and like records.

<u>Bounty Land Warrants</u> were created by the new Continental Congress in a program called Bounty Land Warrants and Pensions and were used between 1776 and 1856. Quite a span of years!

The purpose was to reward persons, usually in the form of land, for serving in various wars. *Land* was what the Government owned, but hard money was hard to come by for this fledgling government. Military *reserves* were set aside, and *reserved for military bounty land warrants* from 1778 to 1816. The land was set aside specifically for these brave and otherwise unrewarded soldiers.

Military *reserves* were set aside for men who joined the service from a particular place. Thus it might be an easy guess that if military land were taken up during this time period, the soldier was probably from the state where the land was reserved for their particular soldiers.

Military Bounty Land Warrants were issued by the Federal government, thus those records would usually be housed with the Federal agency issuing these warrants. But *states* also granted bounty land and these probably are on file with the Secretary of

State, or the state archives of the state issuing these bounty land warrants.

Example: All land below the Green River in Kentucky was reserved for Virginia military men. A block of land in North Tennessee was reserved for North Carolina soldiers. A certain tract of land in Ohio was set aside for Connecticut soldiers, etc. The military reserves map here shows all major tracts.

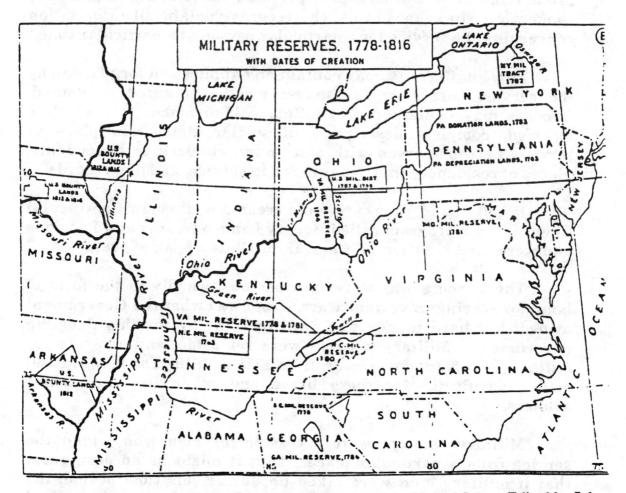

Paullin, Charles O. Atlas of the Historical Geography of the United States. Edited by John K. Wright. Published jointly by Carnegie Institution of Washington and the American Geographical Society of New York, 1932.

Generally the system used to parcel out these lands as military rewards was based on rank served or attained in the military unit. The following are some generalizations for Revolutionary War service personnel:

* 100 acres for each noncommissioned officer or soldier
* 150 acres for an ensign
* 200 acres for each lieutenant and proportionate amounts up to 500 acres for higher ranks up to that of Colonel
* 850 acres for a brigadier general
* 1,100 acres for a major general

Thus we can see that if our ancestor received 100 acres, he probably was a private, or at least below the rank of lieutenant.

It wasn't until 3 March 1855 that Congress passed an act authorizing 160 acres to soldiers regardless of rank. Anyone qualified if they served in the Revolutionary War or took part in any battle during this war. This opened the door for living widows, minor children, and even the still living Revolutionary War veterans to reapply and get more land. If you find evidence that your ancestor acquired 160 acres around 1855, look for a military bounty land warrant.

Congress passed another act in 1856 which extended benefits to naval and marine officers, enlisted men, their widows and minor children. Anyone who served in 1775 and was still alive in 1856 would have been at least aged 90! Thus we might look for elderly grandfathers who married younger women about this time, thus qualifying these young women for benefits. The last widow of a Revolutionary war soldier did not die until 1906. That is 131 years from 1775.

CONGRESSIONAL ACTIONS AFFECTING THOSE WHO SERVED IN THE AMERICAN REVOLUTION

The Congressional Act of 20 May 1775 issued Bounty Land Warrants to military personnel. This first act placed the burden to provide the actual benefits with each individual *state*. By 1818, pensions had been requested in such large numbers that the government was in deep financial trouble. It was about this time that many of the applications were dropped from the rolls. An act in 1821 restored many of these. Numerous records were created with these two distinct acts. Two more acts in 1828 and 1832 opened many more new doors for applications for Bounty Land Warrants to the service men and their widows. These acts for Bounty Land Warrants should be searched and studied when one suspects an ancestor applied for or was granted a Bounty Land Warrant.

Invalid pensions, those pensions which applied for invalid or infirm persons only, were granted as early as 1776. These gave soldiers half pay during their period of disability. Only those who served in the Continental Army (often referred to as Continental Line Soldiers) were eligible. Remember that most of the troops served in their own state's militia and never in the Continental Army.

Many acts were passed, and each seemed to affect our ancestors. These are included here so we can walk our ancestor through the years as they themselves watched (and heard) about these acts being passed by the Congress. After each was written, passed, and word went out across the country's grapevine, one can almost watch and see where the information went by the numbers of applications which came in under the new laws. Good news and bad news traveled fast. One can imagine news of the latest changes being brought into a frontier community which benefited ex-soldiers. Discussions around the courthouse lawn, talk about *who could apply for what,* must have been most interesting. I am sure many applications were made quickly.

PENSION ACTS

<u>26 Aug 1776:</u> Invalid Pensions were granted by Congress for officers and soldiers. Half pay was granted during disability. Both were for Continental Line soldiers only.

<u>24 May 1780:</u> Widows and orphans of officers of the Continental Line were granted half ay for seven years. This act was rescinded in 1789.

<u>21 Oct 1780:</u> This pension act granted pension for life and was only given to officers of the Continental Line.

<u>28 Jul 1789:</u> The federal government assumed responsibility for the states' invalid pensions for Continental Line soldiers only.

<u>3 Mar 1805:</u> Invalid pensions were granted for those disabled since the war from injuries which were incurred *during the war* for Continental Line soldiers only.

<u>10 Apr1806:</u> Invalid pensions were granted and extended to include volunteers, militia, and state troops for service during the Revolutionary War.

<u>18 Mar 1818:</u> This act provided for a pension for *any* soldier who had served for nine months or longer in the Revolutionary War.

These pensions provided that:
* Officers receive $20.00 per month.
* Non-commissioned officers or privates receive $8.00 per month.
* Soldiers were required to relinquish any other pension previously received.
* Claims were to be taken before the District Judge or any court of record for the state or county where the applicant currently resided.
* If a board were satisfied with the applicant's evidence of service as submitted, the application was then sent to the Secretary of War.

* If the claim at this point was considered a legal claim, the applicant was then placed on the pension rolls and notified.

Act of 1820:
This act caused thousands of soldiers to apply who had previously been stricken from the pension rolls. Many who were then applying were rejected. Chaos was created by a then worrisome federal deficit of over $4,200,000. It was reported in February of 1823 that of the 198,880 pensioners who had been admitted and accepted by 4 September 1822, only 12,331 remained on the roll. The office of the Secretary of War was inundated by complaints. A new act was reviewed and quickly passed.

Act of 1823:
This act restored pensions to many who had been dropped. By November of 1823, 17,439 names were on the pension rolls. Many that had been removed were again eligible, but they had to prove their need for aid, thus providing more documents for searching with more information. Considering the numbers pensioners who became eligible, it is very possible that one of them was your ancestor.

Act of 1832:
In a more liberal act, if an officer or enlisted man had served at least two years in service, he would now be entitled to a full pension. The evidence required for acceptability was much less stringent. Many men made applications with little or no evidence presented that they had served. This act *did not* help the genealogist.

4 Jul 1836:
Pensions for widows of Revolutionary War soldiers who were on the pension rolls of 1828 or married during the last term of their service or before 3 November 1783 were granted. Proof of marriage was required.

3 Mar 1837:
A widow was to be entitled to a pension even if she remarried.

3 Feb 1853:
A widow was entitled to a pension regardless of the date of her marriage to the soldier. This brought on a lot of weddings just for the pension.

OBTAINING PENSION RECORDS
AND
BOUNTY LAND WARRANTS

Applications for Revolutionary War pensions and Bounty Land Warrants are contained on 2,670 rolls of microfilm and available for search from several sources. Both master copies of films and the original records are housed at the National Archives in Washington, D.C. There are over 80,000 pensions and bounty land warrant files. Is your grandfather in one of these files?

TYPES OF PENSIONS

There are four different types of military pensions:

* Disability Pensions
* Invalid Pensions for physical disabilities incurred during duty.
* Service Pensions for those who served for a specific amount of time.
* Widow's Pensions for women whose husbands had been killed in war or served for a specific length of time according to the law.

WHAT TO EXPECT TO FIND IN A PENSION FILE

The Pension files are currently housed in 10" by 14" manila envelopes. They contain applications and other records pertaining to claims for pensions or bounty land warrants. There are index cards for these files which have a summary of information about the claimant. There may even be a summary card for those who have no original application papers. These cards provide a cross-reference, using variant spellings of names. It also provides names of the widows who remarried and other pertinent information that can be a tremendous help to the genealogist.

In 1910, pension papers were unfolded by Archives personnel and arranged into *three series*.

1. Approved applications of "survivors".
2. Applications of widows
3. Rejected applications of survivors and widows

By 1912, this project was completed and all the files were consolidated. The card lists contain the following information and symbols.

* The state or organization from which the veteran served
* Name of veteran, widow or applicant
* "s" for survivor
* "w" for widow's pension
* "r" for rejected
* "BLWt" for Bounty Land Warrant

The actual files contain the following:

* One or more post-1800 approved applications
* Affidavits of other veterans (depositions)
* Documentary evidence of service submitted by the applicant (such as discharge certificate, commission, etc.)
* Printed summarization of claimed service
* Property schedules
* Jackets, formerly used to hold application papers before the filing project of 1910-1912 may hold notes of interest
* Certified copies of veteran's service records supplied by State Officials
* Powers of Attorney, or various correspondence
* Letters from genealogists and historians
* Replies from pension officials.
* May contain forms which were sent to the applicant to fill out and return
* Miscellaneous records

WIDOWS' AND CHILDREN'S PENSIONS

As you scan the Congressional acts which affected widows and children's benefits, you can see how many valuable documents could have been created. A widow applying for a pension or bounty land warrant had to submit proof of who she was. Examples of what might be found in her file include: Her name, possibly her maiden name, her age, residence, date and place of marriage, date and place of the death of her husband, a copy of the marriage certificate, or evidence of other marriages, husbands' death date and proof, etc. Requests of children and other heirs or dependents may contain the same type of information. "Other Dependents" could mean an elderly parent or a sibling of whom the veteran was guardian (one who needed care and was completely dependent upon the veteran).

As mentioned previously, it became an accepted custom for a younger lady to marry an older Revolutionary War pensioner about the time the widow's pensions were approved. He could have been a widower, or elderly, and looking for someone to care for him. Or she could have been searching for a steady income.

Pension applications frequently contain documentation which could surprise you. Sometimes the whole family Bible or a page torn from it was sent with the application. After all, there was no photocopy machine around the corner. The government had asked for proof. The Bible was considered proof. What better way than rip the page out and send it in. Affidavits of neighbors, friends, family or others who knew the applicant for years and possibly were witnesses to events were sent with the applications. These pension applications contain concrete information and clues regardless of whether they were denied or approved. The genealogical information found is well worth any time and effort spent in acquiring it.

REJECTED APPLICATIONS

Many applications for both pensions and Bounty Land Warrants were rejected, but they created files for us to search. They might contain one or all of the following:

* Name of veteran
* Age of veteran
* State from which the veteran served
* State and county in which the application was made
* Organization from which the veteran served
* Name of widow if she submitted the application
* File number
* One or more approved pension applications, if they were approved before the last application was rejected

These files may contain application for increase of pension. We must constantly be aware of the various acts and changes in the acts which were in effect when searching for this type of information.

PRE-1800 DISABILITY PENSION APPLICATION FILES

Numerous Revolutionary Veterans applied for or received a disability pension before 1800. A National Archives program created file cards indexing these old applications. These cards contain the following information:

* State from which the veteran served
* Organization from which the veteran served
* Name of veteran

File symbol: "Dis. No Papers" indicates the veteran's original disability pension application and related papers were destroyed. In November of 1800, a fire presumably destroyed all Revolutionary pension and Bounty Land Warrant Applications and related papers. Over 14,000 of these were destroyed. Pre-1800 information has been published in *The American State Papers,* Class 9, Claims (Washington 1834). In 1814, another fire apparently destroyed some of the files submitted *after* 1800.

Though early records were burned in fires of 1800 and 1814, the collection was increased and enhanced in 1873, when the department purchased some records of the pre-federal period from a private collector. Congress ordered military records transferred from the Treasury Department, Interior Department, and State Department and added to the War Department's records. State records from Massachusetts, Maine, Virginia and North Carolina were collected and placed in these files. They have been a great addition to the National Archives records and to the genealogist.

BOUNTY LAND WARRANT FILES

Officer's applications which were submitted prior to the 1800 fire might contain some or all of the following information:

* State or organization from which the veteran served
* Name of veteran
* Symbol "B.L.Wt," followed by the Warrant Number (Bounty Land Warrant)
* Number of acres granted

* Officer's rank
* Date warrant was issued
* Notation "no papers"
* Names of persons, other than the officer to whom the warrant was delivered or assigned are also frequently mentioned.

Some original cards were destroyed after the information was added to the envelope file.

ENLISTED MEN APPROVED PRIOR TO THE 1800 FIRE

Each enlisted man has a separate card file for Bounty Land Warrants. These cards contain part or all of the following information:

* Name of soldier
* Rank
* State or organization from which he served
* Warrant number
* Number of acres granted
* Issue or date of warrant
* Sometimes name of persons to whom the warrant was delivered/assigned

NATIONAL ARCHIVES RECORDS, WITHDRAWN FROM FILES

Between 1894 and 1913, several types of records were withdrawn from the Revolutionary War Pension and Bounty Land Warrant application files. They were removed and sent to specific agencies.

Muster rolls, payrolls, returns, orders, miscellaneous personnel files, lists and papers were sent to the War Department in response to an act of Congress approved in 1892 and 1894. Some lists of Navy veterans were sent to the Naval Department by the Act of 1907.

Diaries, journals, orderly books, account books, and other *bound* records were transferred to the Library of Congress in February of 1909. These records are cross-referenced with notations as to where to find them for any one particular record.

The National Archives responded to the genealogists and historians by providing a section within their holdings called *Selected Records from Revolutionary War Pension and Bounty Land Warrant Application Files.* These contain copies of papers judged to have the most useful genealogical information and have been filmed as series M805.

RELATED RECORDS

Other titles and materials are also available on film such as:

* List of North Carolina Land Grants in Tennessee, 1778-1791 (1 roll). This is in book form also.
* War of 1812: Military Bounty Land Warrants, 1815-1858 (14 rolls)
* Township plats of selected states (67 rolls)
* Records of the United States General Accounting Office, contain:

    · Pension payment books and final payment vouchers,
    · Miscellaneous Treasury Accounts, 1790-1840 (1,170
    · rolls)
    · Ledgers of Payments, 1818-1872 (23 rolls)
    · Day Book, Register's Office of Treasury, 1789-1791 (1 roll)

* Military Service Records, from the War Department Collection of Revolutionary War Records, are also housed in the *Special Records* Collection of the National Archives. They contain:

    · Index to Compiled Military Service Records of Revolutionary War (58 rolls)
    · Index to Compiled Service Records, Revolutionary War Veterans who served in Connecticut (25 rolls)
    · Compiled Service Records of Naval Personnel: Quarter Master General and Military Stores of the Revolutionary War (4 rolls)
    · Compiled Service Records of the American Army of the Revolutionary War (4 rolls)
    · Record books of pay and settlement of accounts for the Revolutionary War (39 rolls)

COMPILED SERVICE RECORDS

Records of *volunteer* soldiers who served in various wars and conflicts have been compiled by National Archives personnel and have card indexes. These show the soldier's presence or absence on specific dates, his rank and organization, term of service, discharge(s), and sometimes the place of enlistment and his birthplace. These records are of great value to us and should be searched. Many ancestors won't show up on a pension file, but often the compiled service records will lead us to the place where they lived or mention an age that can provide a clue found in no other place. Indexes to these records exist. Both the compiled service records and their indexes have been microfilmed.

LOYALIST RECORDS

Sometimes listed as ROYALISTS, an estimated one third of the male population of this country at the time of the Revolutionary War was loyal to George III, King of England. For many of these men, raised from birth to follow the king's dictates, there just didn't seem to be any other way. Many chose to believe the king would prevail and win the war. Others chose to endure defeat rather than renounce their allegiance to the king.

Many thousands of these Loyalists as they were called, migrated north to Canada, or south (even as far as Florida) to escape involvement in the war. They formed their owned political party called the Tory party. If your ancestor was "of age" during revolutionary times and you find no evidence of him in military records, you might try searching Tory, Loyalist or Royalist records.

If your ancestor was a staunch member of the Church of England, or Episcopal Church, he was quite possibly a Loyalist. If your ancestor entered the United States from 1800 to 1825, especially through Canada, after the cause had settled down, he may possibly have been a Loyalist.

Many books and articles have been compiled or written about the Loyalist groups in several states and areas. These publications should be searched.

OTHER CLAIMS

PRIVATE CLAIMS

The series of books called *An Alphabetical List of Private Claims* published by Genealogical Publishing Co. in 1970 contain records of claims made to the U.S. government. Alphabetically arranged, the entries contain:

* Name of the Claimant
* Nature of the object of the claim
* Which Congress, or which Session was involved
* How the claim was presented or brought before the House of Representatives
* Page number of journal on which the petition was recorded
* To what committee of the House the petition was referred
* The number or *date* of the report
* The nature of the report
* How it was disposed of by the Senate
* Date of Act of Congress
* Remarks

Example: ABBOTT, James — Indemnity for property taken for public use: petition, presented to the 21st Congress, 1st session; recorded on page 93 of the journal: referred to the Committee on Claims: Report # 55; Nature of the report was favorable; It was disposed by the House of Representatives as passed; Disposed of by the Senate as passed, date of approval 10 May 1830.

The clues in this one report for claims petitions are remarkable. Study the report and contents. All types of information including clues to identification and location of other records may be found in this work. One may find claims for invalid pensions, military pensions, review claim and pension petitions, claims for goods taken by the military, and other valuable genealogical information. The book is usually found in larger genealogical collections.

SOUTHERN CLAIMS COMMISSION

The Department of Treasury records for Civil War Claims 1871-1880 include 14 rolls of film containing over 22,000 claims heard by the Commission of the Treasury. Civil War Claims are indexed by the name of the claimant and by location. These claims were made by <u>southern residents</u> who were LOYAL TO THE UNION! These records contain interesting historical material as well as genealogical material.

OTHER INDEXES AND REGISTERS

OLD WAR INDEX TO PENSION FILES

From 1815 to 1926 a Pension Index File other than the ones previously mentioned was created. The *Old War Pension Index* file. These records from the National Archives are contained on seven rolls of microfilm.

REGISTER OF U.S. ARMY ENLISTMENTS

Another index or register contains other than wars listed under a definitive title such as the Revolution, Civil, War of 1812, etc. There are 81 rolls of such film from the Department of the Adjutant General's office which are called *Enlistments* covering the years from 1798 to 1914. These should be checked for research materials.

VETERAN'S HOMES

When reviewing military records of a National origin we often forget the veteran's homes, hospitals, etc. These were first created about 1866 to house veterans with disabilities, or of an age where there was no one to care for them. The records are housed with the Veteran's Administration of the War Department. These homes currently are called Veteran's Administration Centers. Currently these records are housed with the National Archives and filed under the classification of Veterans Administrations. Researchers might investigate whether their ancestor received care in one or more of these homes or hospitals.

Example: One of my Civil War ancestors had resided in and around the Chicago, Cook County, Illinois most of his life. I could find no death record for him anywhere in the Cook County area. I received a military record for him and found that he had died in <u>an old soldiers' home</u> in Milwaukee, Wisconsin. I wrote to the Old Soldiers' Home and received the following information: His full name, death date, death place, burial place (in Indiana where he was born), his birthplace, his wife's maiden name (and given name), children's names, their addresses at the time of his death, unit served in during the Civil War, his age, location of next of kin, administrator of his estate (his son in Birmingham, Alabama where I later found his administration papers), and a physical description.

All the information that I had searched for in vain in Cook County, Illinois records, I found in Milwaukee, Wisconsin. Note again that *he had never resided there nor had he any relatives there.* It was just the location of the Old Soldiers' Home.

NATIONAL CEMETERIES AND BURIAL GROUNDS

As previously mentioned, the Old Soldiers' Home in Wisconsin also had a burial cemetery on the grounds. The burial record was recorded and I found my veteran had a marker provided by the Cemetery Services of the Military Branch. Such cemeteries may be called Soldiers Cemeteries as this one was or National Cemeteries.

National Cemeteries have existed since 1861. Any person who has served in the Armed Forces is eligible for burial in these National Cemeteries. Records created are filed with:

> Cemetery Service
> National Cemetery System
> Veteran's Administration
> 810 Vermont Avenue
> Washington DC 20420

These records are indexed by the name of the deceased. The records of burials of soldiers who died between 1861 and 1868 are in the U.S. Soldier's Home Cemeteries. These records contain the soldiers name, military organization and rank, place of enlistment, place of burial, date of death, soldier's age, widow's name, cause of death, and possibly other information.

HEADSTONES

Markers, gravestones, or headstones have been provided by the Federal Government for U.S. veterans since 1879. Records are incomplete, but when they exist often contain the following:

* Name of applicant for headstone (probably NOT the name of the deceased)
* Name of veteran
* Veteran's rank and years served
* Place and date of burial

The National Archives has a card file of these which is indexed first by state, then by county, then by cemetery. It covers the time period from 1870 to 1903.

Some cemeteries may have special sections for veterans. When you find all of a family all together except the father, this may be a clue to military service. And if the grave is in a National Cemetery, you know automatically that some evidence was provided to prove military involvement and that other records will exist.

PRINTED VOLUMES FOR MILITARY RECORDS

Literally hundreds of books and other publications contain military records. Authors have been fascinated with war materials for years. Historians continue to delve into the old records to get new slants on war, the history of war, and records involved with the people who served in these wars. Thus we have printed volumes concerning nearly every aspect of war.

Genealogists, historians, private individuals and groups interested in preserving records have compiled and published lists of items entitled or labeled as some of the following headings or titles. Published lists of veterans, rosters, pensions, bounty land warrants, newspapers, obituaries, cemeteries, annual reports, reports of Commissioners on Pensions, or similar type lists.

Of special interest is the *Official Records of the War of the Rebellion* series of books. They were compiled for both the armies and navies of the war and are indexed by name of soldier or sailor. This and similar type series are available for search for each war and conflict of your research interest.

These lists of books can be searched in card catalogs, lending library catalogs, sales catalogs, Library of Congress catalogs, Periodical Serial Index (PERSI), annual periodical indexes, biographies, bibliographies, etc. One can search these books under the place the ancestor lived, the place the ancestor fought, the place the ancestor enrolled, or was discharged, under the unit name, etc. We might be surprised at what title or heading might contain our ancestor's record in printed form. We just need to look.

WOMEN IN WAR

We think nothing of our young women today standing side by side with men in wartime situations. But this has not always been so. Women did serve, and even fight in all of our wars of record, but most of them were dressed as men and only revealed when wounded (especially early wars). What records survive of this service usually will be in print because of the rarity of the situation.

In the Civil War approximately 400 women served in the military disguised as men (or that is what the records reveal). Many women openly served as doctors, nurses, clerks, laundresses, secretaries, etc. Women were captured and exchanged. The highest rank in the Civil War reached by a woman was First Lieutenant.

Quaker women were leaders in the Abolitionist movement. Their religion defined men and woman as equal. Thus these women learned to handle themselves with great confidence. Married women sometimes followed their men to battle areas.

And then there were other women involved socially with the military — "the other kind," the "camp followers." Sometimes you find items mentioned in the daily journals of officers about these women. For the most part the women who plied their trade are not found in official or unofficial records. If they are, we cannot be sure they used their real names.

PAPERS OF THE CONTINENTAL CONGRESS, 1774 - 1789

The First Continental Congress met on the 5th of September, 1774. Thirteen colonies reported. Georgia did not report. Most of these records are in manuscript volumes and represent our countries earliest history. The creation of the first Department of War took place on the 12th of June, 1776. Records of this first Department of War are scattered throughout committee reports, letters, and comments on the change and growth of the department. The National Archives is the custodian of all of the records created by the Continental Congress.

Military affairs constituted a separate entry in the and can be found at the National Archives in *Records of the Continetal and Confederation Congresses and the Constitutional Convention* (Record Group 360). There are three series of records in this record group. The largest is a 204 roll set entitled *Papers of the Continental Congress, 1774-1789 (series M247)*. Those rolls that contain genealogical information are identified as:

M247-48: Indexes to item 41 on memorials, claims for losses, resignations from military service or similar type services.

M247-54, 55, and 56: Indexes include petitions to Congress, final settlements of accounts, compensation for wartime losses, land titles and grants, exchanges of prisoners of war, etc.

M247-196 Item 184 is a bound, alphabetical index to the Oaths of Allegiance taken by officers in the Continental Army February 1778 through January 1789.

M247-78 through 89: These films contain the state papers for New Hampshire, Rhode Island, Massachusetts, Maryland, Virginia, North Carolina, South Carolina and Georgia.

M247-201 Item 195 contains *Oaths of Allegiance of 1776-1789* with an alphabetical index, Oaths of Allegiance, and Oaths of Office taken by military officers and appointees to public office.

USING MAPS FOR MILITARY RESEARCH

REVOLUTIONARY WAR

When you have identified a Revolutionary War ancestor, the muster rolls and payrolls, and possibly the pension application or Bounty Land Warrant applications may mention at least one battle in which your ancestor took part. This should send you immediately to history books to review (or search for the first time) where these battles took place and what happened. Before long you may at least become a minor student of Revolutionary War Battles.

Maps will help locate your ancestor's unit and involvement. Get as much information as you can. Nothing else helps as much to understand what the people were going through, and the involvement of your ancestor. Maps are available in history books, from genealogical purveyors of books and maps, and from many other sources.

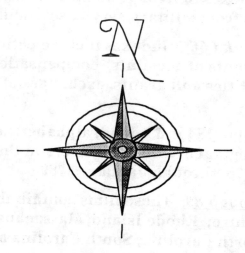

The following two maps are examples. The Battle of Long Island in September 1776 and the Battle of Bunker Hill, 17 June 1775. They give the movement of the units and tell how the battles evolved.

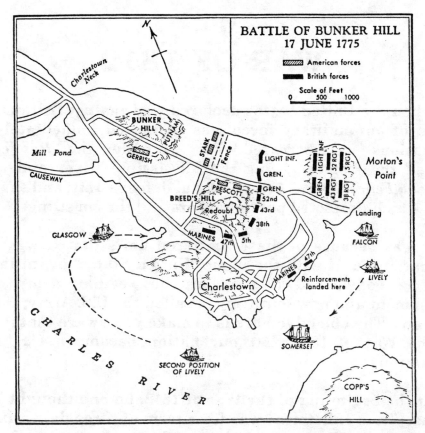

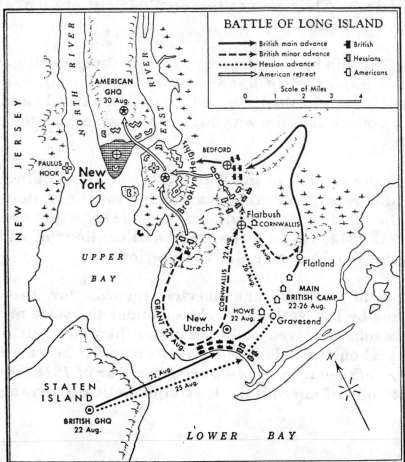

WAR OF 1812

When the United States declared war against Britain in 1812, the size of our military force was increased immediately. New organizations were created. For example: the *Rangers* who protected the frontier along the Mississippi River and adjacent states; *Sea Fencibles*, an Army Coastal defense unit; and the *Flotilla Service* which protected ports, harbors and the coastlines.

It was because of these scattered units that it was decided later that any unit with the name "United States" or initials "U.S." would be considered a part of the regular army military establishment and now our army is called the U.S. Army, U.S. Coast Guard, etc. The objective here is to make you aware that it was not until the War of 1812 that our nation became a U.S. military organization.

At the beginning of the War of 1812, no one thought it would last long. Thus enlistment was for a term of three days, sixty days, or ninety days. Thus we get the reenlistment of men who served their time and reenlisted.

A great number of men served many times during the War of 1812. It is important to know that a man *may have served more than once.* He enrolled, served, was discharged, and enrolled again. In other words the war might be considered a series of short battles.

Also the records of the War of 1812 may be confusing. Some may include records of other wars being fought at the same time such as the Florida and Seminole War of 1812, or the Creek Indian War of 1813-1814. So be forewarned and cautious of which war(s) the ancestor fought during this time period.

Most of the military service records for this war are categorized by the National Archives under the state or area from which the soldier served and then under the unit name or number. The comprehensive index, *Indexes to Compiled Service Records of Volunteer Soldiers who served during the War of 1812* (Series M602) is on 234 rolls of microfilm. It is alphabetically arranged. Each index card gives the name of a soldier, his rank, and the unit or units in which he served. Ther are cross-references for names that appear in the records under more than one spelling. The master indexes are at the National Archives. Copies of microfilm are available through the American Genealogical Lending Library, LDS Family History Centers, or National Archives branches.

There are also the following indexes by state:

Louisiana (3 rolls)
North Carolina (5 rolls)
South Carolina (7 rolls)
Mississippi (22 rolls)

The Index to War of 1812 Pension Application Files (Series M313, 102 rolls) reproduces the faces of the envelopes containing the War of 1812 pension applications. They are arranged alphabetically by name of veteran. Information contained in these files may include: name of veteran, name of widow if she applied, pension applications, bounty land warrants, etc.

Example: One ancestor did not live long enough to apply for a pension, but his widow decided in 1849 to apply for a bounty land warrant. The ancestor served from the State of Tennessee and died there. The widow moved to Platte County Missouri, where she applied for the bounty land warrant and a pension. She received the pension of $8.00 per month, and 60 acres in Berry County, Arkansas as her bounty land warrant. She moved to Arkansas, took up the land, and died there.

The War of 1812 was fought in many locations. The following map may help place some of the battles in your mind and help you follow your ancestor through the battles as well as providing information which may lead you to other records located in the National Archives and in other places.

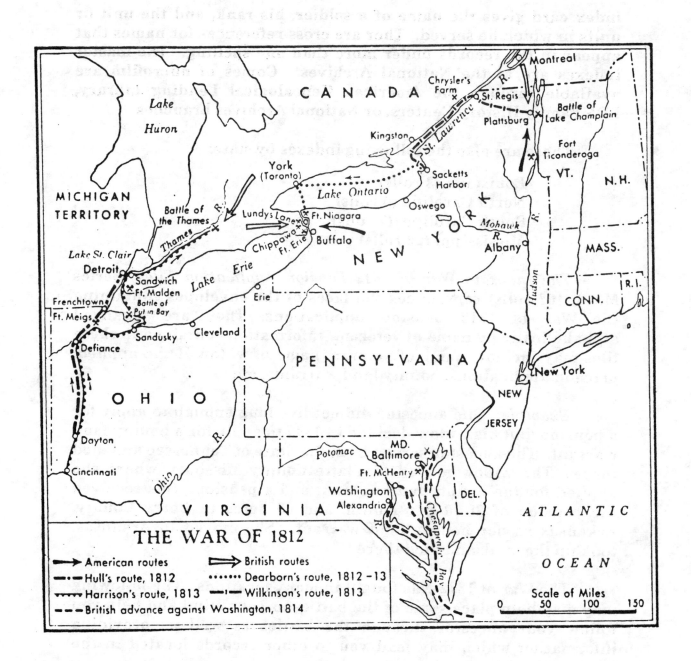

THE WAR OF 1812

American routes → British routes
Hull's route, 1812 ···· Dearborn's route, 1812–13
Harrison's route, 1813 Wilkinson's route, 1813
British advance against Washington, 1814

Scale of Miles
0   50   100   150

INDIAN WARS

Before, during, and after the War of 1812, volunteer units served during times of Indian uprisings. Compiled service records exist for these soldiers for the years 1815-1858 which include service in the following Indian Wars:

* Seminole Indian Florida Wars 1817-1818, 1835-1842, and 1855-1858
* Winnebago War 1827
* Sac and Fox War 1831
* Indian War Texas 1849-1851
* Indian Creek removal 1835-1841
* Other Indian Wars

The War Department did not acknowledge some Indian skirmishes as a bonafide "war" for records' sake. Some, like the following, were fought entirely by volunteers and they (or their heirs) may have received pensions or bounty land warrants for their services. These included:

* Osage War of 1832
* Heatherly War of 1836
* Patriot and Aroostock War of 1838-1839
* Cayuse War of 1848
* And many others

Records regarding this type of service are housed at the National Archives and arranged by state or organization, with regiment, battalion, or company being mentioned in the records. Under each unit the service records are arranged alphabetically. The name of the unit should be known, but by using an index the researcher may find the information fairly easily. Compiled records for Indian wars are available within some states. Examples:
* Alabama: Creek War; Cherokee Removal; Florida Indian Wars
* Georgia: Cherokee disturbances; Cherokee removal
* Louisiana: Florida War; War of 1837
* Michigan: Patriot War

* New York: Patriot War
* North Carolina: Cherokee disturbances; Cherokee removal
* Tennessee: Cherokee disturbances; Cherokee removal

An alphabetical index to volunteer services for Indian Wars 1815 to 1858 are on 42 rolls of film and contains name, rank and unit. This microfilm series in M629. This card file contains the name of disturbance or war, and is cross-referenced for spelling variants.

Volunteers from the state of Alabama for the Creek War are indexed on two rolls of film (M244). The Florida Wars are also indexed. The *Compiled Service Records of Volunteer Soldiers who Served in Organizations from the State of Florida During the Florida Indian Wars, 1835-1958* can be found on 63 rolls of film (M1086).

The Patriot War of 1838-1839 involved Canadian as well as United States citizens. Farmers and artisans alike fought in this war. Federal troops were sent to the frontier in 1838 and troops from all over the country served. Records are compiled for soldiers who served from the state of Michigan (M630, 1 roll) and soldiers who served from the state of New York (M631, 1 roll).

Do you skim this information thinking your ancestor did not fight in these wars? I can report to you that mine did. At the age of 35 my ancestor left the middle of Missouri on horseback to join a unit in Tennessee. He fought in the Seminole Indian Wars. Later, he received a bounty land warrant for land in Wyandotte County, Kansas, and a pension of $8.00 per month until his death. His pension application and bounty land warrant application were found on 32 documents, each containing some genealogical information of value.

THE MEXICAN WAR, 1846 - 1848

War with Mexico was declared on 13 May 1846. It involved regular military and naval units as well as volunteers and militia. Military men were limited to no more than six months of continuous service, while volunteers could enlist for twelve months or until the end of the war. Many of these men would later go on to serve as leaders in the Civil War. Some volunteers had served in earlier Indian Wars. Texas volunteers were retained in the service after the war to protect the frontiers.

The National Archives has compiled service records for the Mexican War (M616) on 41 rolls of film, alphabetically arranged. A card index to these records has also been filmed.

Separate compiled records also exist for the following units:

Mississippi	(M863, 9 rolls)
Pennsylvania	(M1028, 13 rolls)
Tennessee	(M638, 15 rolls)
Texas	(M278, 19 rolls)
Mormon Organizations	(M351, 3 rolls)

The Mormon organizations include the Mormon Battalion. These were volunteers organized at Council Bluffs, Iowa, 16 July 1846. There were approximately 200 men organized into five companies. Many records about the Mormon Battalion exist in the Historical Department Archives of the Church of Jesus Christ of Latter-Day Saints in Salt Lake City, Utah.

Pensions were also given for service in the Mexican War. There is an *Index to Mexican War Pension Files, 1887-1926* on microfilm series T317 containing fourteen rolls of film. There are also *Selected Pension Application Files Relating to the Mormon Battalion, Mexican War, 1846-1848* (Series T1196, 21 rolls).

Campaigns of the Mexican War can be found in history books. You may be surprised to find at least one of your ancestors who served in this conflict.

THE CIVIL WAR *or* WAR OF THE REBELLION *or* WAR BETWEEN THE STATES, 1861-1865

This war was America's most costly. More than 1,000,000 people out of an approximate 31,000,000 Americans lost their lives. This was the largest total number of people lost in any war. It was also one of the longest wars. Only the Revolutionary and Vietnam Wars were longer. This war ended the institution of slavery but did not come to grips with the basic problems of race relations.

President Lincoln's first call for servicemen was issued April of 1861. In this call he asked for 75,000 militia men. Later acts asked for many more. Any adult male of recruitment age was accepted. During the first two years, units were mustered in for short periods of time. After all they did not expect the war to last long. The normal enlistment was from one to three years, or to the end of the war.

Most soldiers served in units formed in their own neighborhoods, from their own counties, and from their own states. A reenlisting soldier may have been assigned to another unit. As units dwindled in numbers, they were disbanded or absorbed into other units. This may make following a unit through the entire war most difficult. Disabled soldiers wishing to stay in service were often assigned to a special group called the Veterans Reserve Corps (VRC). Their records may be found there.

The sheer enormity of numbers may have your head reeling in a very short time when considering Civil War research. In it, 2,261 battles were fought. Over 1,000,000 men lost their lives. There were 16 *Rebel* prisons. In 1887 there were 36,401 headstones and graves counted for *Union* soldiers who died in these 16 prisons. Of those prisoners, 11,599 were known to have been released, but died before they reached their homes, and 12,000 of those who reached home died shortly thereafter. To me these figures are incomprehensible. But on we must go in order to understand how to do genealogical research in Civil War records.

The units in which servicemen served were given a designated number, a state or territory name, and the branch or the armed services.   Some unit designations were called by the name of the officer who formed or commanded a particular company.

Examples:
5th Missouri Cavalry
1st Cavalry—Captain Ward's Battery, Light Artillery.

There are compiled military service records for nearly all soldiers who were accepted for service in the Union Army. Records of enlisted men include information about their age, residence at time of enlistment, occupation and physical description.

Confederate records are also compiled and some are housed at the National Archives. However, many of the Confederate records are available in the individual state.

INDEXES

Separate indexes are available for each state and territory *except* South Carolina which furnished no white troops for the Union Army, but did have some blacks who fought for the Union Army. Be careful when using these indexes prepared by the National Archives staff. We may believe a man served from one state, when he actually served from another. We may need to search several indexes. Microfilmed indexes have been compiled for Union Soldiers for the following States.

Alabama	Florida
Arizona	Georgia
Arkansas	Idaho Territory
California	Illinois
Colorado Territory	Indiana
Connecticut	Iowa
Dakota Territory	Kansas
Delaware	Kentucky
District of Columbia	Louisiana

Maine	Pennsylvania
Maryland	Rhode Island
Massachusetts	South Carolina
Michigan	Tennessee
Minnesota	Texas
Mississippi	Utah Territory
Missouri	Vermont
Montana	Virginia
Nebraska Territory	Washington Territory
Nevada	West Virginia
New Hampshire	Wisconsin
New Jersey	Wyoming (see Washington
New Mexico Territory	Territory)
New York	U.S. Colored Troops
North Carolina	U.S. Volunteers
Ohio	Veterans Reserve Corps
Oregon	

Civil War research can begin with the National Archives, but be sure to check the printed materials about your area. Many have been abstracted and printed in book or periodical form. These may save you time and effort. Indexes are available for most Civil War research.

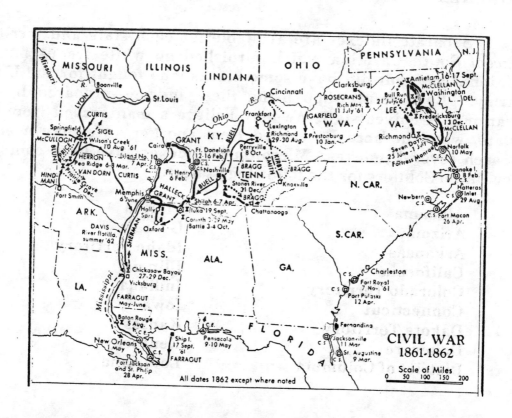

CIVIL WAR
1861-1862

Scale of Miles
0   50   100 150   200

All dates 1862 except where noted

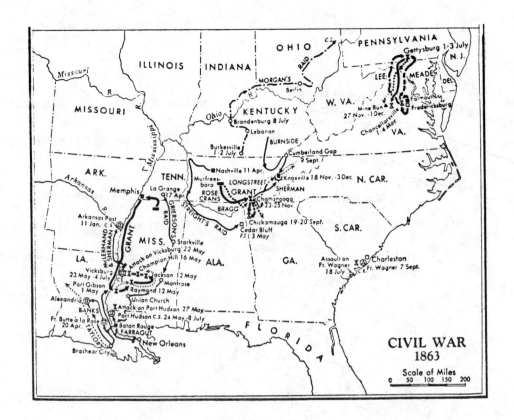

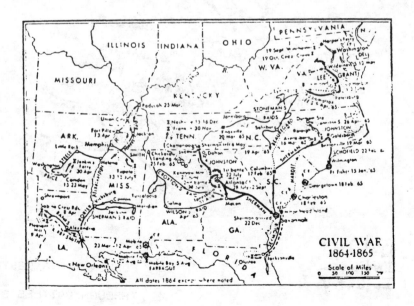

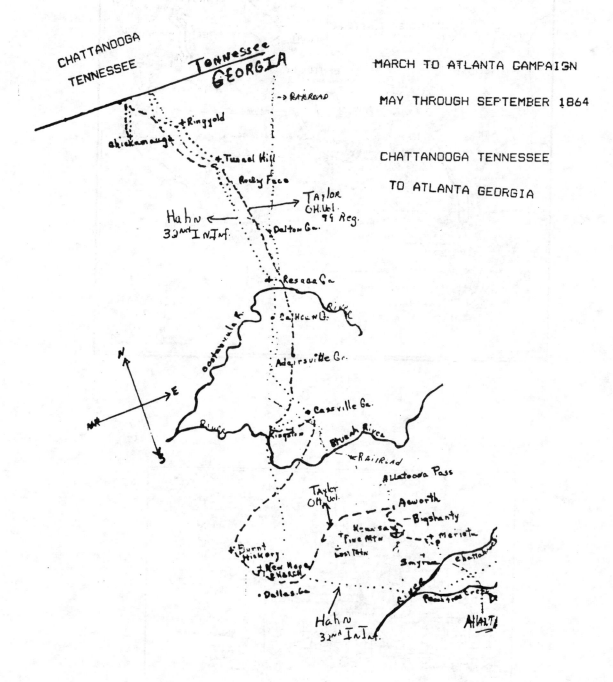

CHATTANOOGA
TENNESSEE

Tennessee
GEORGIA

MARCH TO ATLANTA CAMPAIGN

MAY THROUGH SEPTEMBER 1864

CHATTANOOGA TENNESSEE

TO ATLANTA GEORGIA

FOLLOW TWO ANCESTORS

THROUGH BATTLES BY

UNIT RESEARCH

..... Hahn - 32nd Indiana Infantry

- .- .- Taylor - Ohio Volunteers 99th Regiment

UNION RECORDS

Most of the records we have mentioned previously have been Union Records that is, records for Union Soldiers. Records would be found at the National Archives, at state archives and historical societies, in historical collections, museums, and other repositories. The National Archives films include a *General Index to Pension Files, 1861-1934* in series T288 (44 rolls). These contain pension applications for Army, Navy, and Marine Corps. Each file card in the general index contains the veteran's name, rank, unit, and term of service; names of dependent(s); filing date; application number; certificate number; and the state in which the claim was filed.

There also exist *Indexes to Compiled Service Records of Volunteer Union Soldiers Who Served In Organizations Not Raised By States or Territories* on 36 rolls of microfilm. These indexes are part of the Adjutant General's office records and contain records from the 1780's to 1917. The rest of the indexes are by state where the veteran served.

CONFEDERATE RECORDS

In April of 1865 the Confederate Government abandoned Richmond, Virginia. Some of the military records passed into the hands of the Union Army and were preserved. But many of the Confederate records have not been kept. Confederate pensions were NOT granted by the federal government. For files other than what are mentioned here you might contact:

Museum of Confederacy
1201 East Clay Street
Richmond, VA 23219

In 1903, the United States Secretary of War persuaded the governors of most southern states to lend the War Department the Confederate military records for copying. These records were abstracted by the War Department between 1903 and 1927 with a master index. This index is called *The Confederate Records*. They are filed by state.

Microfilmed indexes of Confederate Army *Volunteers* held by the National Archives are:

Alabama	(M374, 49 rolls)
Arizona Territory	(M375, 1 roll)
Arkansas	(M376, 26 rolls)
Florida	(M225, 9 rolls)
Georgia	(M226, 67 rolls)
Kentucky	(M377, 14 rolls)
Louisiana	(M378, 31 rolls)
Maryland	(M379, 2 rolls)
Mississippi	(M232, 45 rolls)
Missouri	(M380, 16 rolls)
North Carolina	(M230, 43 rolls)
South Carolina	(M381, 35 rolls)
Tennessee	(M231, 48 rolls)
Texas	(M227, 41 rolls)
Virginia	(M382, 62 rolls)

A consolidated index has been created for these Confederate records and arranged alphabetically on 535 rolls of film. This is microfilm series M253. Many additional Confederate service and pension record applications are available from the Adjutant General's office in the individual states.

There are records relating to *Confederate Medical Officers*, indexes relating to *Confederate Soldiers, Sailors, and Citizens Who Died in Federal Prisons and Military Hospitals in the North* on 1 roll of film. There are also narrative reports of *Confederate States Army Casualties* (7 rolls), and *Records of the War Department Relating to Confederate Prisoners of War* (145 rolls), and other like records.

Amnesty papers: Case files exist of *Applications from former Confederate Soldiers for Presidential Pardons, 1865-1867*. These are indexed by state from which the veteran served and are on 72 rolls of film. These are most interesting in that each is different, usually handwritten, and each seems to tell an individual story.

Civil War genealogical study can be both fascinating and rewarding. Each step seems to lead to another. Our interest seems to grow with each step. Civil War battles are especially interesting to follow when your ancestor fought in these specific battles.

The National Parks Service, the National Archives, and The Federation of Genealogical Societies and their volunteers are currently undertaking a mammoth project of inputting a complete computerized list of both Union and Confederate soldiers who served in the Civil War. Plans are to make the database available on CD-ROM.

SPANISH AMERICAN AND MODERN WARS

From the time of the Spanish American War (1898) and through the more modern wars the records are more detailed and complete. However, they are more difficult to access. Records are restricted to immediate family members under the Right to Privacy Acts. Most of the records are housed at:

The National Personnel Records Center
Military Personnel Records
9700 Page Blvd.
St. Louis, MO 63132

Spanish American War records have been separately indexed and filmed for each state. The indexes are on 24 rolls (M871), *General Index to Compiled Service Records of Volunteer Soldiers who Served During the War With Spain.* The service records are on 126 rolls in series M872, *Index to Compiled Service Records of Volunteer Soldiers who Served During the Philippine Insurrection.* Both sets of records have descriptive pamphlets.

More recent war records are also housed at the same St. Louis facility and are accessible by the veterans themselves and/or the immediate family. The genealogical data is abundant but for the sake of privacy the information is not released to unrelated persons.

MILITARY RECORDS RECORDED AND HOUSED BY THE STATES

Many state archives house military records for their individual states. These have been donated through the years by counties, private individuals, historical societies, genealogical societies, and others interested in preserving valuable military records. For example, The Florida State Archives (Bureau of Archives and Records Management, R. A. Gray Building, Tallahassee, FL) houses all of Florida's State military records from the 1820's through the 1970's. These early records include state militia rolls from the Seminole Indian wars and the Civil War. Many states retain similar types of records.

CENSUSES

There are two notable censuses which deal with military enumeration. The first, taken in 1840, has proven to be of great value through the years by both genealogists and historians. It provides us with the name of the veteran, his age and residence. This 1840 census has been abstracted and is printed for easy use and access.

All that remains of the 1890 Federal Census other than three rolls of microfilm is the *Special Schedules Enumerating Union Veterans and Widows of Union Veterans of the Civil War*. These schedules listed the name of the veteran, his age, rank, company or regiment, enlistment and discharge dates, length of service, address, and disability (if any).

BATTLE RESEARCH

During the Civil War, the Federal Army (Union) named their battles after the closest waterways such as bays, creeks, lakes, rivers, etc. The Confederates named battles referring to land locations. Thus we have the *same battles listed under different names*. History books can be confusing with these different names of battles.

The Battle of the Shiloh Meeting House [Confederate name] and the Battle of Pittsburgh Landing [the Union name] are the same battle. Sharpsburg (a town, thus being a Southern Confederate battle name) and Antietam (a creek, thus being a Union Battle name) are one and the same. Manassas (a town) and Bull Run (a river) are both the same battle. So, as we can see, history teaches us many things which we need in the study of genealogy.

Keep in mind that military records were created, not for the genealogist or historian, but for military purposes. We can profit greatly from the use of the records that were made and preserved for other purposes. The National Archives and the indexing programs through the years have been a considerable help. Now genealogists need only to learn *what* is there, *how* to find those records, and *what we can expect to find* in those records. They contain our ancestors' names and genealogical connections from generation to generation which we can sometimes find in no other way.

When we have identified in military records a battle in which our ancestor took part, battle research can begin. Many publications, mostly historical in nature, furnish great detail about military and naval conflicts.

The hand-drawn map previously included on page 48 illustrates two ancestors, not from the same state, nor from the same unit, who were found to have been involved in the March to Atlanta, Georgia in the Summer of 1864. History books told of the march and how it began at Chattanooga. Battles were fought along the way, and towns were mentioned, helping me plot these two gentleman on the map. The Chickamauga Battleground National Park contains many monuments erected to the memory of the troops who marched through the area.

Lists of men who fought in the battles can be found at the visitors' centers and museums at the battle sites. When you stand near a monument to a unit in which your ancestor served, you feel a silent wonder. Locating the units of your ancestors will bring a thrill and help in finding information. Check these out on your next trip or write for information.

The best advice I can give is to *ask*.

FORMS AND WHERE TO OBTAIN THEM

As usual, when working with government agencies, one needs to fill out forms – usually in triplicate. Your request must be submitted on NATF Form #80 (the form for Military, Pension and Bounty Land Warrant Files or Copies of Veterans' Records). To request information from the National Archives on military, pension, and bounty land warrant files you may write to the following address:

General Reference Branch (NNRG)
National Archives and Records Administration
7th and Pennsylvania Avenue NW
Washington, DC 20408

Photocopies of records relating to service in World War I, World War II, or subsequent service can be requested from:

National Personnel Records Center
Military Records
National Archives and Records Administration
9700 Page Blvd
St. Louis, MO 63132

MILITARY ORGANIZATION

For those of us with no military experience whatsoever, the structure may prove difficult to understand at first. But the organizational structure of any group follows a definite chain of command. The military structure of our armies is (in descending order of rank):

ARMY
      CORPS
            DIVISION
                  BRIGADE
                        REGIMENT
                              BATTALION
                                    COMPANY
                                          PLATOON
                                              SQUAD

Battalion: A ground force consisting of three or more companies or similar units.

Brigade: A unit consisting of several regiments, squadrons, groups or battalions.

Company: A subdivision of a Regiment or Battalion (small group of soldiers). In the Navy this may be a ship's crew, including officers.

Corps: Any organized unit consisting of officers and men — or officers alone. It consists of two or more divisions. During the Revolutionary War, a corps was one of the nine military subdivisions of the Continental Army.

Division: A major administrative and tactical unit. It is larger than a regiment or brigade and smaller than a corps.

Militia: A body of men enrolled for military service, called out periodically for drill and practice, but used in actual service only in emergencies. They are citizen soldiers as distinguished from professional soldiers.

Platoon: A military unit consisting of two or more squads or sections having a common headquarters.

Regular Army: The permanent United States Army, in peace and in war time.

Regiment: A ground unit consisting of two or more battalions.

Squad or Squadrons: A squad is a small unit of men (usually ten or more) with a sergeant and a corporal in command. A squadron can be a Naval Fleet unit, or an armed cavalry unit consisting of two or more troops and support units.

Troop: Armed Cavalry of two or more platoons and a headquarters group.

Unit: An organized body of soldiers of *any size*. A division of a larger body.

Volunteer: One who enters service of his own volition rather than by draft or conscription.

Conscripts: Recruits who were drafted for military service. A compulsory monetary payment was provided by the government for enlistment of men in war time. Conscripts is the name used earlier; we now call such soldiers "draftees."